PIANO · VOCAL · GUITAR

SHAKIRA.

ISBN 978-1-4803-9492-6

HAL•LEONARD®
CORPORATION
7777 W. BLUEMOUND RD. P.O. BOX 13819 MILWAUKEE, WI 53213

Visit Hal Leonard Online at
www.halleonard.com

CAN'T REMEMBER TO FORGET YOU

Words and Music by SHAKIRA MEBARAK,
ROBYN "RIHANNA" FENTY, JOHN HILL, DANIEL LEDINSKY,
THOMAS EDWARD PERCY HULL and ERIK HASSLE

Bm
Em
ry. Well, you make me feel, yeah, you got a hold on me; I nev - er
ry. The way he makes me feel like, the way he makes me feel, I nev - er
A
D
C♯dim
4fr
met some - one so dif - f'rent. Oh, here we
seemed to act so stu - pid. Oh, here we
Bm
Em
go. You're part of me now, you're part of me. So
go. You're part of me now, you're part of me. So
A
N.C.
B5
where you go, I fol - low, fol - low, fol - low, oh.
where he goes, I fol - low, fol - low, fol - low, oh.
Oh

A5
E5
G5
F♯5
oh, oh, oh oh, oh, I can't re - mem-ber to for-get you.
B5
A5
G5
Oh oh, oh, oh oh, oh, I keep for -
D5
C♯dim
B5
get - ting I should let you go. But when you
A5
E5
G5
F♯5
look at me, the on - ly mem - o - ry is us kiss - ing in the moon - light.

To Coda
B5
A5
5fr
G5
3fr
Oh oh, oh, oh oh, oh, I can't re-
1
N.C.
Bm
Em
mem-ber to for-get you.
Ooh, ooh, ooh ooh
A
D
C♯dim
4fr
Bm
ooh. I can't re-mem-ber to for-get you.
Ooh,
Em
A
D
C♯dim
4fr
ooh, ooh ooh ooh.

2
N.C.
Bm
mem - ber to for - get you. I'd rob and I'd kill to
Em
A
D
C♯dim
4fr
keep him with me; I'd do an - y - thing for that boy. I'd
Bm
Em
A
give my last dime to hold him to - night; I'd do an - y - thing for that
1
D
N.C.
2
D
N.C.
B5
D.S. al Coda
boy. I'd boy. Oh

CODA
E5
G5
F#5
oh, oh, I can't re - mem - ber to for - get you.
B5
A5
E5
But when you look at me, the on - ly mem - o - ry is us
G5
F#5
B5
kiss - ing in the moon - light. Oh
A5
G5
N.C.
oh, oh, oh oh, oh, I can't re - mem - ber to for - get you.

EMPIRE

Words and Music by INA WROLDSEN
and STEVE MAC

C
Fm/A♭
B♭
F
And my heart _ beats
like the
C
Fm/A♭
B♭
C
Fm/A♭
em - pires _ of the world u - nite.
We are _ a - live,
and the
B♭
C
Fm/A♭
stars _ make love to the u - ni - verse.
You're my wild - fire _ ev - 'ry sin - gle night.
B♭
C
Fm/A♭
We are _ a - live,
and the

B♭
stars make love to the u - ni - verse.
F
And you touch me, and I'm like,
1
and I'm like, and I'm like,
C
Fm/A♭
ooh,
B♭
ooh.
And I'm like,
C
Fm/A♭
ooh,
B♭
ooh.
And I'm like,
C
Fm/A♭
ooh,

B♭
C
Fm/A♭
To Coda
B♭5
ooh. And I'm like, ooh.
2
C
Fm/A♭
and I'm like, and I'm like, ooh,
B♭
C
Fm/A♭
B♭
ooh, we are a - live, ooh. And I'm like,
C
Fm/A♭
B♭
ooh, ooh, we are a - live.
3

C
Fm/A♭
B♭
A♭5
4fr
I'm just gon-na raise my head, wel-come to the
B♭5
3
C5
3fr
fi - nal edge, and I'm gon-na fall. I'm just gon-na
A♭5
4fr
B♭5
raise my head and hold you close like the
C
Fm/A♭
B♭
em - pires of the world u - nite. We are a - live,

C
Fm/A♭
B♭
and the stars make love to the u - ni - verse. You're my
wild - fire ev - 'ry sin - gle night.
We are a - live,
and the stars make love to the u - ni - verse. And you
F
touch me, and I'm like, and I'm like, and I'm like,
N.C.
D.S. al Coda
CODA
B♭5

YOU DON'T CARE ABOUT ME

Words and Music by NASRI ATWEH,
CHANTAL KREVIAZUK and ADAM MESSINGER

C♯m A B6/9 C♯m A B6/9
sour tongue. I loved you on-
pour the wine. The bot-tle's emp-
C♯m A B(add2)
-ly, but there's no re-cip-ro-ca-tion.
-ty, but there's no con-sum-ma-tion.
A C♯m
Be-fore you came a-long, it was all beau-ti-ful. I have noth-ing left
A
in my heart, in my soul. Should have nev-er helped you be-come so pow-er-ful,

B(add4)
C♯m A B
but I saw a champ-pi-on in your eyes. You don't
C♯m A B
care a-bout me. If you did, you would let me go.
C♯m A B F♯m C♯m A B
And you will, e-ven-tu-al-ly, 'cause you just don't
C♯m A B
care a-bout me. You don't care if I die.

C♯m A B C♯m A B
If you did, you would have spared my life. I say it
To Coda
1
F♯m C♯m A B
con - fi - dent - ly, that you just don't care a - bout me. You
2
F♯m
care a - bout me. Oh, ba - by, how we used to dance.
E6 D♯m7
I could - n't sep - a - rate from your hands. Now they don't e - ven

G♯
4fr
play that song an - y - more.
You don't care a - bout
N.C.
me. Don't care a - bout me, no, don't
You don't care a - bout me, no, don't
1
2
D.S. al Coda
care a - bout me.
care a - bout me.
CODA
care a - bout me.
C♯m
4fr
B6
C♯m
4fr
B6

DARE
(La La La)

Words and Music by SHAKIRA MEBARAK, JAY SINGH,
RAELENE ARREGUIN, LUKASZ GOTTWALD, MATHIEU JOMPHE-LEPINE,
MAX MARTIN, HENRY WALTER and JOHN J. CONTE, JR.

N.C.
Leg - go.
Leg - go.
Leg - go.
Leg - go. All of my life, too late
till you showed up with per - fect tim - ing. Now here we are, we rock it.

Our fin - gers are stuck in the sock - et. It's just the na - ture, a game.
Get read - y and we'll do it a - gain. Let's not re - cov - er from the hang - o - ver.
When your eyes got me drunk, I was so - ber. Is it true that you love me?
I dare you to kiss me with ev -
C♯m
G♯m
B
F♯
C♯m
4fr

G♯m
4fr
B
F♯
-'ry - one watch - ing. It's truth or dare on the dance floor.
C♯m
4fr
G♯m
4fr
B
La, la, la, la, la, la, la, la, la, la la, la, la, la, la,
Truth or
F♯
C♯m
4fr
G♯m
4fr
la, la, la, la. La, la, la, la, la, la, la, la, la, la,
dare on the dance floor.
B
F♯
N.C.
To Coda
la, la, la, la, la, la. I dare you.

Leg - go.
Leg - go.
Of all the mil - lions on the plan - et,
you're the one who's keep - in' me on it.
D.S. al Coda
You know I like you like no - bod - y's bus'- ness,
your blue Span - ish eyes are my wit - ness.
CODA
C♯m
4fr
G♯m
4fr
B
Is it true that you love me?
I dare

F♯
C♯m
4fr
G♯m
4fr
B
you to kiss me. I dare you to touch me. It's truth or
F♯
dare on the dance floor, dance floor, dance floor, dance, dance, dance, dance,
6
da, da, da, da, da, da, da, da, d, d, d, d, d, d, d, d, d, d, d, d, d, d.
3
C♯5
4fr
La, la, la, la, la,
G♯5
4fr
B5
F♯5
la, la, la, la, la, la, la, la, la, la, la, la, la, la.

C♯m
4fr
G♯m
4fr
B
La, la, la, la, la, la, la, la, la, la, la, la, la, la, la,
F♯
N.C.
la. I dare you.
Leg - go.
Leg - go.
Leg - go.
Leg - go.

CUT ME DEEP

Words and Music by SHAKIRA MEBARAK,
NASRI ATWEH, MARK PELLIZZER, ALEX TANAS,
BEN SPIVAK and ADAM MESSINGER

E♭
3fr
F
Gm
3fr
Bul - lets are fly - in'; this time I can't shield them.
Climb up the moun - tain so high we can see them.
E♭
3fr
F
San - ta Ma - ri - a, I know how it hurts.
Send me to plum - met with sav - ag - ing words.
Gm
3fr
F/A
F7
B♭
'Cause you cut me deep.
D7
Gm
3fr
F/A
Your words are like steel.

B♭
D7
Gm
3fr
F/A
And now I can't sleep
B♭
D7
Gm
3fr
'cause
F/A
B♭
D7
I'll nev - er heal.
Gm
3fr
Gm11
1
2
3
I am
3

Cm
3fr
Dm
E♭
3fr
cov - ered in scars. Like a rose with - out thorns,
Cm
3fr
Dm
my de - fens - es are gone. No one's
Gm
3fr
F
Cm
3fr
out there to warn. If there's love in your heart,
Dm
E♭
3fr
let me leave now in peace. You know you
3

Cm
Dm
Gm
took it too far. 'Cause
F
N.C.
you cut me deep.
Your words are like steel.
And now I can't sleep

B♭
D7/F♯
Gm
F/A
'cause I'll nev - er heal.
B♭
D7
Gm
Gm11
Oh,
B♭
D5
Gm
F/A
you cut me deep, you cut me so deep.
B♭
D5
Gm
You cut me deep, you cut me so deep.

F/A
B♭
D/F♯
You cut me deep, you cut me so
Gm
F/A
B♭
deep.
You cut me deep,
D5
Gm11
you cut me so, so, so, so...
B♭
D5
Gm

F/A
B♭
D5
5fr
You cut me deep, you cut me so
Gm
3fr
F/A
B♭
deep.
D5
5fr
Gm
3fr
F/A
B♭
D5
5fr
Gm
3fr
Gm11
You cut me deep, you cut me so...

23

Words and Music by SHAKIRA MEBARAK
and LUIS FERNANDO OCHOA

Am
G/B
C
- ly. I used to think that there was no God. But then you looked at me with your blue
- ing 'cause I was cer - tain that things would-n't change. But then you came and I saw you smil -
G/B
F
eyes and my ag - nos - ti - ci - sm turned in - to dust. How well you know
- ing just like an an - gel, so beau - ti - f'lly strange. And then you touched
C
G
me, that I don't care if the rest don't. It does-n't mat - ter to me,
me; it's like you were made for me, oh, like it was all meant to be,
Dm
C/E
F
no. Oh, oh, and as long as you love
oh. And I was sure that you would love

C
Dm7
F
me, as long as we still have each oth - er...
me, and that we'd al - ways have each oth - er.
C
Dm
F
G
I knew we had some - thing from the mo - ment I met you.
C
Dm
F
G
And I knew we had some - thing; no one thought it could be true.
C
Dm
F
G
Hey, do you be - lieve, do you be - lieve in des - ti - ny?

C Dm F G
'Cause I do, as I did then, when you were on - ly twen - ty - three.
C G/B Am7 F
Ba - da - dap - bap, ba - da - dap - ba. Ba - da - dap - bap, ba - da - dap -
C G/B
ba. Ba - da - dap - bap, ba - da - dap - ba,
1
Am
oh, oh.
2
Am7 F Dm7
ba, oh, oh. I al - ways thought that I was fine, but I was wrong.

G
C
G7/B
It was you, that one piece I was miss-
Am
Dm7
- ing. And I could do with-out you, but it'd be no fun.
G
C
G7/B
I found you; life was sud - den - ly eas-
Am
F
- y. There ain't no wor-ries now, there ain't no feel-ing down.

G5 C5 Dm F G
3fr
I knew we had some - thing from the mo - ment I met you.
C5 Dm F G/B
And I knew we had some - thing; no one thought it could be true.
C Dm F G
Hey, do you be - lieve, do you be - lieve in des - ti - ny?
C Dm F C5
'Cause I do, as I did then, when you were on - ly twen - ty - three.

THE ONE THING

Words and Music by SHAKIRA MEBARAK,
NASRI ATWEH and ADAM MESSINGER

* *Melody is written an octave higher than sung.*

Bm7
E
A
I can't ex - plain the way it feels. I could
I can't ex - plain the way it feels. I could
F♯m7
Bm7
E
trip on my own words. I made mis - takes; that much is clear,
choke on my own words. Some - times it seems like it ain't real,
A
F♯m7
Bm
but I made it here, my love. Yeah, I
but you're real - ly here, my love. Yeah, you're
Dm
made it here, my love.
real - ly here, my love.
A
E
You are the one thing that I got right.
mf

F♯m7
D(add2)
A
It's a fick - le world, yeah, it's a fick - le world. You turn the dark -
E
F♯m7
D(add2)
- ness in - to sun - light. I'm a luck - y girl, yeah, I'm a luck - y girl.
A
E
F♯m7
And if I mess up ev - 'ry - thing some - day, I won't
D(add2)
A
E
To Coda
hide my head in shame, 'cause you are the one thing that I got right,

F♯m7
D5
5fr
1
A
right, right, right.
(Ay,
E
F♯m7
D(add2)
ay, ay.) One thing I got right.
A
E
F♯m7
(Ay, ay, ay.)
D(add2)
One thing I got right.
2
A
Ev - 'ry time I see you smile,

E
F♯m
ev - 'ry time I hear you laugh, ba - by, you're bring - ing your
D(add2)
A
E
sun - shine o - ver my way. You are that lit - tle dream I had since I was a child.
F♯m
D
A
My fair - y tale comes true when I look at your face. I may not be
E
F♯m
D6
here for - ev - er, but it - 'll be a long road to - geth - er.

A
E
Bm
I al - read - y know we're gon - na be fine, fine, fine.
Dm
D.S. al Coda
We're gon - na be just fine, fine, fine.
CODA
F♯m
D5
5fr
N.C.
A
'cause you are the one thing that I got right. And if I mess
E
F♯m7
D(add2)
up ev - 'ry - thing some - day, I won't hide my head in shame,

A
E
F♯m7
'cause you are the one thing that I got right, 'cause you are the one
D5
5fr
N.C.
A
E
thing that I got right. (Ay, ay,
F♯m7
D(add2)
A
ay.) One thing I got right. (Ay,
E
F♯m7
D(add2)
N.C.
ay, ay.) One thing I got right.

MEDICINE

Words and Music by SHAKIRA MEBARAK,
HILLARY LINDSEY and MARK BRIGHT

B(add4)
C#m7
4fr
Asus2
Fall - ing a - part,
I need a shock
straight to my heart.
E
B(add4)
Asus2
Both:
No one would want to be in my shoes right now, oh.
B(add4)
E
Female: I don't reach for the bot - tle of whis - key.
No,
Male: Straight on the rocks.
B(add4)
C#m7
4fr
you won't see me pop-ping the pills.
'Cause if I want the pain to go a - way
Male: Pop pop pop pop-ping the pills.

Asus2
Both: in a sec - ond, make it fade, you're the on - ly thing that will. You're my
E
B(add4)
med - i - cine, med - i - cine, my my my med - i - cine, med - i - cine,
To Coda
Asus2
my my my med - i - cine.
E
B(add4)
C♯m7
4fr
Male: You know, you're an ex - pert at com - pli - cat - ing things.
Female: That's how I'm wired.

Asus2
E
B(add4)
Male:
Be - lieve me, it's no fun. But you make a war seem like such an eas -
C♯m7
Asus2
E
- y game.
Female: Kiss me and my ar - gu - ments come un - done.
Both: Down in the trench - es,
4fr
B(add4)
C♯m7
Asus2
you are the white flag. Make me sur - ren - der; want you so bad.
E
B(add4)
Asus2
Female: Ba - by, don't stop what you start - ed. Don't ev - er be done, oh.
Both:

B(add4)
D.S. al Coda
Both: I
CODA
Asus2
med - i - cine.
Female: You
E
make it all bet - ter, bet - ter.
B(add4)
You make me feel whole.
C♯m7
4fr
Both: You make it all bet - ter, bet - ter.
You
Asus2
make me feel whole.
E
Female: I don't reach for the bot - tle of whis -

B(add4)
- key. No, you won't see me pop-ping the pills. Both: 'Cause if I
C♯m7
4fr
Asus2
want the pain to go a-way in a sec-ond, make it fade, you're the on-ly thing that will.
E
You're my my med-i-cine, med-i-cine, my my my
B(add4)
Asus2
med-i-cine, med-i-cine, my my my med-i-cine.

E
You make it all bet - ter, bet - ter. You
B(add4)
C♯m7
4fr
make me feel whole. You make it all bet - ter,
1
Asus2
bet - ter. You make me feel whole. You
2
Asus2
E
make me feel whole. Female: You're my my med - i - cine.

SPOTLIGHT

Words and Music by SHAKIRA MEBARAK,
HILLARY LINDSEY and MARK BRIGHT

B5
C5
G5
D5
leaves her old boy-friend and crum-bles in his arms.
here be-cause you want me and not for what I make.
B5
C5
D
Hey, they'd bet - ter know,
And if they wan-na make me pay
if there is a price to pay
C
D
now, then go on, 'cause lov-ing you was nev - er
now, the game is on, 'cause in the end, you know I
C
G
D
wrong.
won.
Here is my life in the spot - light,

G/B
C
G
D
the spot - light.
And it's hurt-ing my eyes 'cause it's so bright,
G/B
C
G
D/A
so bright.
But you are the link I
G/B
C
G
D
was miss - ing that I could-n't find,
and I would-n't give you up, e - ven if I
1
C
end up blind.
Been
2
C
end up blind.
And ev-'ry cam - 'ra flash my way

D
Em
and ev-'ry word on ev-'ry page, well,
C
they can say what-ev-er they want to, 'cause what we've got is just so real
D
Em
C
that they can't change the way I feel, 'cause I would do it all a-gain for you.
G
D
G/B
C
Here is my life in the spot-light, the spot-light.

G
D
G/B
C
And it's hurt-ing my eyes 'cause it's so bright, so bright.
G
D/A
G/B
C
But you are the link I was miss-ing that I could-n't find,
G
D
1
C
and I would-n't give you up, e - ven if I end up blind.
2
C
G5
3fr
D5
5fr
B5
C5
3fr
end up blind.

BROKEN RECORD

Words and Music by SHAKIRA MEBARAK
and busbee

* *Recorded a half step lower.*

Dsus
Csus2
3fr
Dsus
- ly mu - sic I can't do with - out.
There can't be an - y doubts now.
We're
G5
3fr
G/F♯
Em7
Csus2
3fr
just too far a - head to look be - hind
and a - bove the
Dsus
G
D
good and bad.
I need you to be - lieve in my word.
Em7
G/B
C
I feel like a bro - ken rec - ord.
And I've told you

D
C
D
sev - en hun - dred times: I don't need to keep look - ing; my search is done.
G
D
Em7
Can you put your trust in my word? I sound like a bro -
G/B
C
D
- ken rec - ord. And I've {said it / told you} sev - en hun - dred times:
To Coda
C
D
G5
3fr
I don't need to keep look - ing; you are the one.

Your hands that have no mercy are also my best friends,
Em7
and I can get lost climbing on your legs that never end.
Dsus
G5
3fr
I found the perfect
Em7
distance between my body and you, and that is, no
Dsus
Csus2
3fr
distance, dear, if that's all right with you.
They said we wouldn't make

Dsus
G5
3fr
G/F♯
it, but look at how we've beat - en all the odds.
Em7
Csus2
3fr
Dsus
D.S. al Coda
I just need you to be a - ware that...
CODA
D
Em7
- ing; you are the one. I just want you to take a leap of faith.
G
C
I know it's eas - y to make all the same mis - takes. But I

G/B
Am7
D6
won't this time. No, not this time.
G
D
Em7
I need you to be - lieve in my word, I sound like a bro -
G/B
C
D
- ken rec - ord. And I've said it sev - en hun - dred times:
C
Dsus
I don't need to keep look - ing; you are the one.

G5
3fr
A doz-en ic - y sum-mers were lead-ing me to you.
Em7
Dsus
I had to hear the li - ars to rec-og-nize the truth.
G5
3fr
Re - mem-ber the first Christ - mas? It al - most seemed un -
Em7
Dsus
G5
3fr
true. You prom-ised that you'd al-ways be with me, and I prom-ised, too.
rit.

NUNCA ME ACUERDO DE OLVIDARTE

Words and Music by SHAKIRA MEBARAK,
JOHN HILL, DANIEL LEDINSKY,
THOMAS HULL, ERIK HASSLE
and JORGE DREXLER

A
D
C
que no hay cie - go pe - or
que él que no quie - re
que no hay sor - do pe - or
que él que no quie - re o -
Bm
Em
ver. He-me a-quí ven - ci - da
y ca - si con - ven - ci - da que in - ten -
ír. Es - toy a - quí ven - ci - da
y ca - si con - ven - ci - da que no hay
A
D
C♯dim
4fr
tar - lo es i - nú - til.
Y di - go
na - die más i - dio - ta.
A - quí que
Bm
Em
yo, ¿qué pa - sa con - mi - go?
Mi pe - or cas - ti - go es que a -
yo mue - ro por tu bo - ca
en la bo - ca mí - a, y lo in -

A
N.C.
B5
don - de vay - as, sa - bes, sa - bes que voy yo.
ten - to to - do, to - do, to - do, to - do y no.
Oh,
A5
5fr
E5
G
F♯m
oh, oh, oh, oh, oh. Nun - ca me a - cuer - do d'ol - vi - dar - te.
B5
A5
5fr
G5
3fr
Oh, oh, oh, oh, oh, oh. Nun - ca a - pren -
D
C♯dim
4fr
B5
A5
5fr
dí co - mo de - jar - te ir.
Mi mun - do gi - ra a - sí, al - re - de -

E5
G
F♯m
B5
dor de ti, só - lo me a - cuer - do d'u - na par - te. Oh,
A5
To Coda
G5
5fr
3fr
1
N.C.
oh, oh, oh, oh, oh. Que no me a - cuer - do d'ol - vi - dar - te.
Bm
Em
A
Ooh, hoo, hoo, hoo, hoo. Que no me a -
D
C♯dim
4fr
Bm
Em
cuer - do d'ol - vi - dar - te. Ooh, hoo, hoo, hoo, hoo.

A
D
C♯dim
4fr
2
N.C.
cuer-do d'ol-vi-dar-te. Po-
Bm
Em
A
drí-a men-tir, ma-tar o mo-rir, in-clu-so al-go mu-cho pe-
to-dos me di-cen que no des-per-di-cie que el tiem-po les da la ra-
D
C♯dim
4fr
Bm
Em
or. For-zar el des-ti-no, per-der el ca-mi-no con
zón. Ya lle-ga-rá el dí-a que ha-brá o-tro en mi vi-da, que
A
1
D
N.C.
2
D
N.C.
D.S. al Coda
tal de no per-der tu a-mor. Y
me quie-ra más y me- jor.

CODA
E5
G
F♯m
oh, oh. Y no me a - cuer - do d'ol - vi - dar - te.
B5
A5
5fr
E5
Mi mun - do gi - ra a - sí, al - re - de - dor de ti, só - lo me a -
G
F♯m
B5
A5
5fr
cuer - do de u - na par - te. Oh, oh, oh, oh,
G5
3fr
N.C.
oh, oh. Y no me a - cuer - do d'ol - vi - dar - te.

LOCA POR TI

Words and Music by SHAKIRA MEBARAK,
CARLOS HERNANDEZ, JOSEP BELLAVISTA,
JUAN CLAPERA and ALBERTO HERRERA

* *Recorded a half step lower.*

G D G
me so - ñar que to - da - vía es - tás a - quí.
con - ti - nuar, e - bria y so - ñan - do a - quí,
Em G D
Aún quie - ro se - guir lo - ca por ti.
sa - bien - do que es - toy lo - ca por ti.
A Bm
Si - go so - la a - quí en es - te bar, me fal - ta
G D A
to - do si fal - tas tú. I - ma - gi - no tu cuer -

To Coda
Bm
G
D
A/C♯
-po a - quí, con la lu - na a con - tra - luz. Me que - da - ré,
Bm
Em
G
be - bien - do es - ta co - pa a tu sa -
1
D
lud.
2
D
lud.
G

D
G
D.S. al Coda
CODA
D
A/C♯
Y no me i - ré
Bm
Em
G
D
sin an - tes brin - dar a tu sa - lud.
Em
D/F♯
G
D
Me be - bo es - ta co - pa a tu sa - lud.
rit.